W9-BFL-699

# Cat Mummies

# Cat Mummies

by Kelly Trumble
*Illustrated by* Laszlo Kubinyi

SCHOLASTIC INC.
New York Toronto London Auckland Sydney

The assistance of Sue D'Auria, Consultant, Department of Ancient Egyptian, Nubian, and Near Eastern Art, Boston Museum of Fine Arts, in reviewing the text and illustrations is gratefully acknowledged·

Quotation from Juvenal's *Satires,* translated by Jerome Mazzaro.
Copyright © 1965 by the University of Michigan.
Published by the University of Michigan Press. Used by permission.

No part of this publication may be reproduced in whole or in part, or stored in a retrieval system, or transmitted in any form or by any means, electronic, mechanical, photocopying, recording, or otherwise, without written permission of the publisher. For information regarding permission, write to Clarion Books, a Houghton Mifflin Company imprint, Permissions, Houghton Mifflin Company, 215 Park Avenue South, New York, NY 10003.

ISBN 0-590-26695-0

Text copyright © 1996 by Kelly Trumble.
Illustrations copyright © 1996 by Laszlo Kubinyi.
All rights reserved.
Published by Scholastic Inc., 555 Broadway, New York, NY 10012,
by arrangement with Clarion Books,
a Houghton Mifflin Company imprint.
SCHOLASTIC and associated logos are trademarks
and/or registered trademarks of Scholastic Inc.

12 11 10 9 8 7 6 5 4 3          9/9 0 1 2 3/0

Printed in the U.S.A.          24

First Scholastic printing, January 1998

To Art
—*K.T.*

For my family: wife Suzanne and
daughters Gabriella, Martina, and Natalia
—*L.K.*

# Contents

1  From Totems to Gods                                    1

2  Cat Worship                                            7

3  A Second Chance at Life                               16

4  Bubastis                                              25

5  Persian Conquest                                      32

6  Death of a Religion                                   38

   Appendix

      *Human Mummification*                              45

      *Some Animals and the Gods They Symbolized*        47

      *A Chronology of Ancient Egyptian History*         48

      *Museums*                                          49

   Notes                                                 50

   Names and Terms                                       52

   Selected Bibliography                                 54

   Index                                                 56

# CHAPTER 1
## From Totems to Gods

In the summer of 1888 an Egyptian farmer was working in the desert near the town of Beni Hasan. One day he dug a hole and accidentally made an incredible discovery. Just under the surface of the desert lay thousands and thousands of cat mummies. They had been lying there, undisturbed, for more than two thousand years.

Why did the ancient Egyptians mummify so many cats?

Animals were a big part of religion in Egypt from prehistoric times. Thousands of years before the pyramids were built, before Egypt became one country, the people were divided into clans. Each clan had a sacred symbol, or totem. The totem was usually an animal. As a rule clan members did not kill or eat their totem animal.

Why were certain animals chosen to be totems? Perhaps the clan members chose an animal because it helped them to survive—for example, ibises ate poisonous snakes. Perhaps the clan admired a certain quality in an animal, such as the strength of a bull. Or perhaps they were afraid of a particular animal and thought it might not harm them if they worshiped it.

When war broke out between clans, the winning clan demanded respect for its totem. First one clan rose to power, then another. Eventually a nation was built, and

many totems were held sacred. All along the Nile people revered cats, ibises, hawks, beetles, and other animals.

When the ancient Egyptians began to believe in gods, these gods were not just spirits. The Egyptians believed that gods must have bodies to live in. Sometimes the gods chose to live in the bodies of sacred animals. A particular god would choose a particular animal because they shared some of the same characteristics. For example, Anubis, the god of tombs, lived in a jackal's body because jackals often prowled around tombs.

At first a single animal was chosen to be the body where the god could live. This animal lived in luxury in the temple of its god. Priests fed and cared for the temple animals. Diodorus Siculus, a Greek historian who lived in the first century B.C., reported that temple cats and ichneumons[1] (the Greek name for African mongooses) were fed pieces of bread mixed with milk, or pieces of raw fish from the Nile. Those who had the privilege of feeding the animals wore special emblems, and the people they met bowed to them in respect.

Diodorus also wrote about how the caretakers collected money to use for the animals' food. If an Egyptian had a child who had lived through a serious illness, he made a vow to the gods. To fulfill this vow, the Egyptian shaved his head and weighed his hair. Then he donated an amount of gold or silver equal to the weight of his hair.

The temple animals were thought to be the vessels of the gods. As such, they were treated with care and respect. But the animals themselves were not actually worshiped as gods.

Eventually some people began to confuse the sacred animals with the gods themselves. The cat or crocodile in the temple was no longer just a vessel for a god. It was an actual god. And so was every other cat or crocodile.

Animal worship was especially popular in the Late Period, from 712 to 332 B.C., and beyond. The people treated sacred animals with fanatic devotion.[2] Diodorus reported that anyone caught killing a sacred animal was put to death. It didn't matter whether the animal was killed accidentally or on purpose. If anyone happened to find a dead animal, he backed away from it in horror, mourning its death and declaring his own innocence at the same time.

Around 60 B.C., Diodorus saw just how fanatical the Egyptians could be about their sacred animals. He saw a Roman soldier in Egypt accidentally kill a cat. At that time the Roman Empire was the most powerful empire ever. The Egyptians had every reason to be afraid of the Romans. But that didn't stop a mob from gathering at the soldier's house. The pharaoh Ptolemy XII sent officials to plead for calm. But the mob's devotion to cats was overwhelming. They killed the Roman.

# CHAPTER 2
## Cat Worship

The ancient Egyptians held cats sacred from the earliest times. Cats protected the food in houses and granaries from rats and mice. They also killed asps and other poisonous snakes.

Cats played many roles in Egyptian mythology. In one story, a cat saved the world from darkness and evil. The ancient Egyptians believed that when the sun set, a battle was fought between Ra, the sun god, and Apep, the serpent of darkness. Every night Ra turned into a cat and fought the evil Apep. Every night he chopped off the serpent's head. Then in the morning the victorious sun could rise in the east. But Apep was immortal. So every night he came back to life to fight the sun god again.

One member of the cat family, the lion, was the sacred animal of two Egyptian goddesses, Sekhmet and Bastet.[1] Each goddess was portrayed with a woman's body and a lion's head. But the goddesses were exact opposites.

Sekhmet was violent and angry. She was the goddess of war and diseases. She stood for the destructive, burning power of the sun.

Bastet was kind. She was the bringer of good fortune and good health. She stood for the good power of the sun, the power to make things grow.

The destructive Sekhmet continued to have a lion's head. But eventually the gentle Bastet's lion turned into a cat. More and more often Bastet was pictured with a woman's body and a cat's head. The cat became her sacred animal.

One legend said that Bastet was once stung by a scorpion and saved by the sun god, Ra. If an Egyptian was stung by a scorpion, he would reenact that event in Bastet's life. First he cried out, as Bastet had: "O Ra! Come to thy daughter, whom a scorpion has bitten on a lonely road!" Then he answered in Ra's words: "Do not fear, do not fear, my splendid daughter; behold, I stand behind thee. It is I who destroy the poison that is in all the limbs of this cat." By putting himself in Bastet's place and reciting this spell, the Egyptian believed he would be saved by Ra, just as Bastet had been.

The main temple of Bastet was in the city of Bubastis. When Sheshonk I became pharaoh around 945 B.C., he built Bubastis into an important city. The cult of Bastet then became popular all over Egypt. This was the time when cat worship began to rise to a fanatical level.

Artisans made thousands of small bronze sculptures of cats. They sold them to people who worshiped Bastet. These worshipers offered the bronze cats at temples and shrines and hoped for an answer to their prayers.

Cat amulets became popular with young married women. A woman would buy an amulet (a magical charm) showing a cat and her kittens and hang it on the wall. Then she prayed to Bastet for the same number of children as the number of kittens on the amulet.

Herodotus, a Greek historian who lived from around 484 to 425 B.C., traveled all over Egypt. He wrote that when a fire broke out, the Egyptians did not show any concern for the property being burned. Instead, they protected cats. Men stood around the fire to make sure no cats ran into the burning building.[2] If a cat perished in the fire, the Egyptians deeply mourned its death.

If a cat died a natural death in a house, Herodotus reported, all those who lived in the house mourned the loss by shaving off their eyebrows.

The reverence an ancient Egyptian felt toward a cat did not end when the cat died. It was important to bury a sacred cat with the respect it deserved. And that respect included mummification.

# CHAPTER 3
# A Second Chance at Life

According to legend, when the god Osiris reigned over the earth with his wife, the goddess Isis, he civilized the Egyptians. He gave them laws. He taught them how to plant and harvest crops. He was a kind and well-loved ruler.

His brother Set was jealous. He wanted the crown for himself. Set conspired with seventy-two men to kill Osiris. First, he secretly measured Osiris. Next, he built a beautiful wooden chest just the right size for his brother. Then, he invited Osiris to a feast. At the feast Set promised to give the chest to whomever it fit exactly. Each of the seventy-two conspirators tried to lie in it, but not one of them fit exactly. Osiris was the last to try. As soon as he lay in the chest, the men slammed the lid. They nailed it shut. Then they threw the chest into the Nile.

Isis searched for the chest and found it near the mouth of the river. She tried to hide it, but Set found it. He cut up Osiris's body into fourteen pieces and scattered them all over Egypt.

Isis searched for the pieces of Osiris's body. With the help of the other gods she put the pieces together, embalmed the body, and wrapped it in linen. Then she fanned the body with her wings.[1] And Osiris became alive again. From that time on he was the god of the dead.

Osiris died, but he came back to life. The ancient Egyptians thought, "Perhaps people can do that too." After all, Osiris died against his will, and people die against their will. Osiris got a second chance at life. So the Egyptians prepared their dead for a second chance at life.

The ancient Egyptians believed that within a living person was a special life force. They called it the *ka*. As long as a person was alive, his ka stayed within his body. When he died, his ka left him.

The Egyptians believed that the ka would come back to the body and give it new life, just as Osiris had been given new life. But first the ka needed to find the body it belonged to. If the body was decayed, the ka couldn't recognize it. So the Egyptians learned to preserve the body with mummification.

Embalmers treated the body with salts and wrapped it in linen. This stopped the body from decaying. If the body didn't decay, then it could still be recognized, and its ka could find it again. A statue of the dead person, called a ka statue, might be entombed with the mummy. Then the ka could live in the statue if the mummy was destroyed.

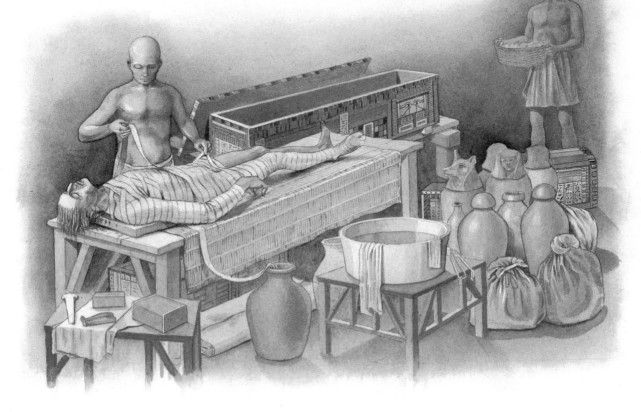

Cats were treated in much the same way. A cat had its ka too. Its body had to be preserved so that its ka could find it again someday. Then the cat could come back to life.[2]

Sometimes a cat was mummified in an elaborate way. The body was wrapped in strips of linen that had been dyed in two colors. The linen strips were woven together to form beautiful patterns. The head was covered with a mask made of a material similar to papier-mâché. Pieces of linen were sewn on the mask to look like eyes. Ears were made from the midribs of palm leaves, set in a natural position.

Other cats were mummified in a simple way. They were rolled up only in a piece of plain linen. But the rolling was done with the care and respect that a sacred animal deserved.

Many cat mummies were buried in coffins. These were made of bronze or wood. Some coffins were shaped like cats. Others were rectangular boxes. Sometimes bronze ka statues were mounted on top of the boxes. Sometimes the boxes had a cat face painted on top. The eyes might be made of crystal and gold, with black obsidian pupils.

Cat mummies were buried in cemeteries created especially for cats. There were cat cemeteries at Beni Hasan, Thebes, and other towns where Bastet was worshiped. But the most famous cat cemetery was in the city where Bastet was especially revered: Bubastis, in the Nile Delta.

# CHAPTER 4
# Bubastis

The city of Bubastis was the center of cat worship in ancient Egypt. It was founded in prehistoric times, perhaps by the clan whose totem was the cat. Tel Basta, near the modern town of Zagazig, is the site of the ruins of ancient Bubastis.

Herodotus thought Bastet's temple in Bubastis was the most beautiful temple in Egypt. It sat on an island, with only its entrance connected to land by a narrow passage. Around the island flowed water from the Nile in channels a hundred feet wide. While the rest of the city had been raised up by embankment over many years, the temple was left alone. So an Egyptian walking around Bubastis could look down on the temple from anywhere in the city.

The temple was made of stone. It was square, with a low wall built around it. Tall trees surrounded the temple's shrine. In the center of the shrine stood a statue of Bastet. Sacred cats were kept near the statue of their goddess.

The building of the temple was begun in the Fourth Dynasty (which began around 2600 B.C.). This was also when the great pyramids were built. Edouard Naville, the Swiss Egyptologist who excavated the temple in 1891, found in the temple the names of Cheops and Chephren,[1] the pharaohs for whom the two largest pyramids at Giza were built.

Amenemhet I, a pharaoh of the Twelfth Dynasty (which began around 2000 B.C.), left his name on the temple too. His inscription read, "He erected his statue to his mother Bastet. . . ."

But in spite of this inscription, Bastet was not yet the most important goddess in the city. She became the most important in the Twenty-second Dynasty (which began around 945 B.C.), when Sheshonk I made Bubastis a major city. His son Osorkon II started to reconstruct the temple, which had been ruined over the centuries. Osorkon III finished the temple and dedicated it to Bastet. This was the temple Herodotus saw.

Bubastis was also the home of a huge cemetery for cats. Because the cat goddess Bastet became the most important deity in Bubastis during the Twenty-second Dynasty, that was probably when the cat cemetery was created too.

Herodotus reported that when cats died anywhere in Egypt, they were taken to Bubastis, mummified, and buried in the cat cemetery. However, Naville's excavation showed that Herodotus might have been wrong. Naville found cat bones piled up in large underground pits. The walls and the floors of the pits were made of bricks or hardened clay. A furnace had been built near each pit. The furnace bricks were blackened from fire. The bones in the pits were mixed with ashes and charcoal.

All this evidence suggested to Naville that in Bubastis cats were cremated. Naville found no evidence that cats were mummified there. But mummification and burial was the rule at other cat cemeteries, such as the one at Beni Hasan.

Some Egyptologists believe that cremation was unlikely because the Egyptians believed so strongly in preserving the body after death. Perhaps the cat bones were burned by accidental fires or acts of vandalism. Whatever the cause, many cats met this fate. In just one of the pits at the cemetery, Naville found over 720 cubic feet of cat bones.

If a room filled with cat bones is 12 feet long and 10 feet wide, the bones would have to be piled up six feet high to equal the number of bones in that one cemetery pit. Imagine how many cats it would take to fill such a space!

Herodotus also witnessed the festival held each year in honor of Bastet. He wrote that it was the most popular festival in Egypt, attended by 700,000 men and women, plus many children. They sailed down the Nile from all parts of Egypt.

The atmosphere on these boats was like a carnival. Some of the men played pipes, while some of the women played castanets. The others sang and clapped their hands. When they came to a town along the banks, some of the women left their boats and went ashore to dance with the women of the town.

The festivities continued like this all the way down the Nile to Bubastis. There the people celebrated with a feast and sacrifices to Bastet. More wine was drunk during this festival than during the whole rest of the year.

The Hebrew prophet Ezekiel lived in the sixth century B.C., when the worship of Bastet and her festival were at their most popular. In the Bible Ezekiel mentions Bubastis, which he calls Pi-beseth, in chapter 30, verse 17: "The young men of Aven and of Pi-beseth shall fall by the sword; and these cities shall go into captivity." Ezekiel believed that Bastet's followers would be captured because they worshiped a pagan god.

In the sixth century B.C. the Egyptians were indeed captured. According to legend, animal worship was one reason for their downfall.

# CHAPTER 5

# Persian Conquest

When Cyrus the Great became king of Persia around 558 B.C., he wanted to conquer all the ancient empires and create one great empire. He was almost successful. When he died in 529 B.C., his armies had conquered Media, Lydia, Babylon, and other empires. But he had not conquered Egypt.

Cyrus's son Cambyses was the successor to the throne. Cambyses wanted to pursue his father's dreams of conquering Egypt. After all, the Nile Valley was wealthy and powerful. It would be an important addition to the Persian Empire. Cambyses set out to conquer Egypt in 525 B.C.

But Cambyses faced one big obstacle. His army was on the eastern border of Egypt, and the Egyptian army outpost at Pelusium was fifty-six miles away. And every one of those miles was across the desert. There were no towns and, more important, no sources of water. How could Cambyses lead his army safely to Pelusium?

Luck was with Cambyses. While he was wondering how to get through the desert, the Egyptian pharaoh Amasis had an argument with Phanes, a mercenary working for the Egyptian army. Phanes decided to switch sides. He went to Cambyses and revealed important Egyptian military secrets. And he told him how to cross the desert.

On Phanes's advice, Cambyses asked for help from the Bedouins, nomadic Arabs of the desert. The Arabs stationed camels across the desert between the Persian army and Pelusium. The camels carried skins filled with water, enough for the Persian army to cross the desert safely.

In the meantime, the pharaoh Amasis died. His son Psammetichus III became pharaoh. The new pharaoh camped with his army at Pelusium to wait for the arrival of the Persians.

The battle was fierce. Both sides knew they had a lot to lose. If the Egyptians were defeated, they would have to live under the rule of the Persians. If the Persians were defeated, they could not retreat through the desert. They would be captured or killed.

36

But Cambyses had a plan. He knew about the Egyptians' devotion to their sacred animals, and he decided to use that against them. His army collected all the cats they could find. Then they released them, along with dogs, ibises, and other sacred animals, at the front of their lines.

The Egyptians were paralyzed. They could not use their weapons against the Persians, because they might kill or injure a cat instead. The army fled from the field. Cambyses took Pelusium.

Cambyses then conquered the rest of Egypt, thus fulfilling his father's dream. The Persian Empire was the greatest empire that had yet been built. It lasted about two hundred years, until Alexander the Great conquered it and the Ptolemies began their rule over Egypt.

## CHAPTER 6
# Death of a Religion

Cambyses wasn't the only one who didn't respect the ancient Egyptians' religion. Many Roman writers made fun of the animal worship they saw in Egypt. Juvenal, who was born in the first century A.D., wrote:

*What won't these mad Egyptians use for Gods?*
*One district worships the green crocodile,*
*another ibises gorged full on snakes,*
*and in another, apes are still the style. . . .*
*Here cats, there riverfish are thought divine, dogs,*
*  too! . . .*

By the second century A.D., Christianity was becoming more and more widespread. Clement of Alexandria was a Christian theologian and educator. He described the beauty of the Egyptian temples: "The halls are surrounded with many pillars; and the walls gleam with foreign stones, and there is no want of artistic painting; and the temples gleam with gold, and silver, and amber, and glitter with parti-colored gems from India and Ethiopia; and the shrines are veiled with gold-embroidered hangings."

But what he found inside did not impress him. When a priest pulls back the veil to show a visitor the god of the temple, Clement wrote, "he will give you a hearty laugh at the object of worship. For the deity that is sought, to whom you have rushed, will not be found within, but a cat, or a crocodile, or a serpent of the country, or some such beast unworthy of the temple, but quite worthy of a den, a hole, or the dirt. The god of the Egyptians appears a beast rolling on a purple couch."

Over the next few centuries Christianity rose, and the ancient Egyptian gods were worshiped less and less. The temples of the gods crumbled. Then, in the seventh century A.D., Arabs conquered Egypt, and their religion, Islam, became the main religion of the Egyptian people. Cats were no longer held sacred. The ancient cat mummies, so carefully preserved, so repectfully buried, lay at rest for more than a thousand years.

The resurrection of the cat mummies near Beni Hasan on that summer day in 1888 was probably not what the ancient Egyptians had expected. Unfortunately, no archaeologist was there that day to make scientific observations. But an eyewitness reported that laborers from the nearby village excavated the cat cemetery themselves. They found hundreds of thousands of cat mummies buried in pits. Each pit contained twenty layers of cat mummies. Now, for the first time in more than two thousand years, they were exposed to the light of day.

Some of the mummies were in poor shape. They were simply black lumps with a few bones or clumps of fur. But many of the mummies looked as if they had just been buried yesterday. Some were wrapped in beautiful two-color woven strips of linen. Some had faces covered with a thin layer of gold.

Children from the village came to the site every day. They dug up the best mummies they could find. These they took down to the bank of the Nile, where they sold them to tourists passing by. Sometimes the children played with the mummies on the way to the riverbank. Or sometimes the children fought with each other and used the mummies as weapons, which made the mummies fall apart. Skulls and bones and pieces of fur and mummy cloth littered the path.

But the sad story of the resurrection of these cat mummies doesn't end here. The scavengers barely made a dent in the huge cemetery. The rest of the mummies were shipped to Liverpool, England, to be auctioned off for fertilizer. The first load weighed nineteen tons. It sold for 3 pounds 13 shillings and 9 pence per ton, or about $18 for a whole ton of cat mummies.

The second shipment was sold one week later. This shipment contained nine tons of cat-mummy pieces. The bones were sold first, for 5 pounds 17 shillings and 6 pence per ton, or about $29 per ton. These bones were also used as fertilizer. Cat-mummy heads were sold separately, with the prices ranging from 42 cents to $1.09 each. One cat-mummy body without the head sold for less than two dollars.

It was a sad ending for these noble cats once thought to be the vessels of the gods.[1] Unfortunately, many Egyptian antiquities met a sad fate in the nineteenth century. Around the beginning of that century Napoleon Bonaparte, emperor of France, commissioned a huge study of Egypt and its ancient monuments. When this study was published a few years later, it triggered an interest in Egypt's ancient wealth all across Europe. Tourists, amateur archaeologists, and natives ransacked ancient monuments for treasure to collect or sell. In this rush for gold, jewelry, and statues, many tombs and mummies were vandalized or destroyed.

Napoleon's men also discovered the Rosetta Stone. Its inscriptions provided the key to deciphering hieroglyphics in 1822. The new ability to read hieroglyphics made scientists more interested in Egyptian archaeology. Now much more could be learned about life in ancient Egypt than ever before. Over the next few decades a desire to preserve and learn from the ancient monuments slowly replaced the looting. After the discovery of Tutankhamen's tomb in 1922, the Egyptian government began to limit the number of antiquities that foreigners could take out of the country. Eventually, everything excavated in Egypt became the property of the Egyptian government.

Many cat mummies have been excavated in Egypt or rescued from looters, and they can be found in museums around the world. The species of cat that lived in ancient Egypt, that was so reverently mummified and buried, is an ancestor of today's cat. Perhaps your cat is a descendant of one of these ancient, sacred animals.

# Appendix
## HUMAN MUMMIFICATION

In very early times, centuries before the pyramids were built, the Egyptians buried their dead in the hot sand of the desert. The bodies were not placed in coffins or wrapped in bandages, so the sand pressed against them. The sand dried out, or desiccated, the bodies by absorbing all the water from them. Since water is needed for decomposition, the buried bodies were perfectly preserved.

The ancient Egyptians would have noticed these mummies preserved by nature, because shifting sands or wild animals would have exposed them. The Egyptians did not yet understand that desiccation was the reason the bodies did not decompose. But perhaps these natural mummies encouraged their belief in an afterlife.

Eventually the wealthier Egyptians could afford to bury their dead in coffins and tombs. But then the bodies were no longer in contact with the sand. They quickly decomposed. By then the preservation of the body was a fundamental part of Egyptian religion. So the Egyptians had to find an artificial way to preserve a body.

At first embalmers tried putting the body in a fetal position and wrapping it in linen bandages that had been soaked in resin. In the Fifth Dynasty a layer of plaster was added over the bandages. The dead person's features could be molded in the plaster so that the person could be recognized. But the body inside decayed anyway.

Eventually someone realized that moisture caused decay. So the body had to be dried out before wrapping. First the internal organs had to be removed, since they decayed the quickest. The embalmer made an incision in the left side of the body. Through this incision he removed the lungs, stomach, intestines, and liver. Usually these were mummified separately and stored in four jars, called canopic jars, which were buried in the tomb with the mummy. Sometimes the organs were wrapped up and put back in the body or placed between the mummy's legs.

The heart was left in the body because the Egyptians believed it was the seat of intelligence. If the heart was accidentally removed, the embalmer put it back in its proper place.

Sometimes the brain was left in the skull, but often it was removed and discarded. One way of doing this was to remove the brain through an incision in the nape of the neck. Another method was to insert a tool in one nostril, break the ethmoid bone at the top of the nostrils, and scoop out the brain through this hole.

Then the body was ready for desiccation. The embalmer used natron, a natural salt that absorbs moisture. The cavity left in the abdomen when the organs were removed was cleansed and then packed with natron. More natron was piled on the body until it was completely covered.

The body was totally desiccated in forty days. Then the embalmer removed it from the natron, washed it, and let it dry. He stuffed the body with resin-soaked linen, or sometimes sawdust, lichen, or even onions! Since the desiccation caused the body to shrink, the stuffing filled it out again to a more lifelike appearance. The embalmer sealed the incision and plugged the nostrils and ears with wads of linen. Then he covered the body with resin.

Now the mummy was ready to be wrapped. This required hundreds of yards of linen in many layers around the body. Amulets and jewelry were placed between the layers of linen to protect the body in the afterlife. Ritual ceremonies were performed during the wrapping, which took fifteen days to complete.

Sometimes a mask was placed over the head and shoulders of the mummy. Most masks were made of linen and plaster, which hardened and then were painted to resemble the deceased. Masks of gold and jewels were made for royal mummies. The famous mask of Tutankhamen is made of solid gold inlaid with lapis lazuli, carnelian, quartz, obsidian, turquoise, and colored glass. It weighs more than 24 pounds.

When the mask was put in place, the mummification was complete. The entire process took at least seventy days. Finally, the mummy was placed in a coffin and was ready for burial.

# Some Animals and the Gods They Symbolized

baboon, ibis — Thoth, god of wisdom and writing

cat — Bastet, goddess of the beneficial power of the sun

goose — Geb, god who personified the earth

hawk — Ra, the sun god; Horus, the sky god and son of Osiris and Isis

hippopotamus — Taweret, goddess of childbirth

jackal — Anubis, god of funerals and embalming

scarab beetle — Khepera, god of the morning sun

snake — Buto, goddess of Lower Egypt

vulture — Nekhebet, goddess of Upper Egypt

# A Chronology of Ancient Egyptian History

| | |
|---|---|
| around 3100 B.C. | Menes unites Upper and Lower Egypt into one country. Memphis is founded and becomes his capital. |
| around 2570 B.C. | Cheops (Khufu) rules Egypt. The Great Pyramid of Cheops, the largest pyramid at Giza, is built. |
| around 2550 B.C. | Chephren (Khafre) rules Egypt. The Sphinx is carved. The second-largest pyramid at Giza is built. |
| around 2500 B.C. | Mycerinus (Menkaure) rules Egypt. The third and smallest pyramid at Giza is built. |
| around 1480 B.C. | Thutmosis III reigns. Egypt is at the height of its power. |
| around 1350 B.C. | Tutankhamen reigns. His tomb survives intact until discovered in 1922. |
| around 945 B.C. | The Libyan Sheshonk I takes over the Egyptian throne and makes Bubastis a major city. |
| 525 B.C. | Cambyses, son of Cyrus the Great, conquers Egypt and adds it to the Persian Empire. |
| 332 B.C. | Alexander the Great conquers Egypt and founds the city of Alexandria. |
| 304 B.C. | Ptolemy I rules Egypt. He begins the Ptolemaic Period that ends with Cleopatra. |
| 30 B.C. | Cleopatra commits suicide. Octavian (later called Augustus Caesar) claims Egypt for the Roman Empire. Egypt is now a Roman province. |
| A.D. 395 | The Roman Empire divides in two. Egypt is part of the Byzantine, or Eastern Roman, Empire. |
| A.D. 642 | Arabs conquer Egypt. Egypt becomes a Muslim state. |

# MUSEUMS

In the United States you can see animal mummies at the following museums. Some museums also have mummy X rays.

Berkeley, California
*Phoebe Hearst Museum of Anthropology*

Boston, Massachusetts
*Museum of Fine Arts*

Chicago, Illinois
*Field Museum of Natural History*

*Oriental Institute Museum of the University of Chicago*

Detroit, Michigan
*The Detroit Institute of Arts*

Kalamazoo, Michigan
*Kalamazoo Public Museum*

Memphis, Tennessee
*Institute of Egyptian Art and Archaeology*

Philadelphia, Pennsylvania
*The University Museum of Archaeology and Anthropology*

Pittsburgh, Pennsylvania
*Carnegie Museum of Natural History*

San Diego, California
*San Diego Museum of Man*

San Jose, California
*The Rosicrucian Egyptian Museum*

Washington, D.C.
*National Museum of Natural History*

# Notes

## 1. From Totems to Gods

1. Ichneumons were revered for keeping the crocodile population in the Nile low by destroying crocodile eggs. Diodorus reported that ichneumons also killed full-grown crocodiles, but this is hard to believe, considering the bizarre way he said it was done: An ichneumon would hide in the mud near sleeping crocodiles. Then, when a crocodile yawned, the ichneumon would leap into its mouth and run down its throat into its belly. The ichneumon would chew through the belly, killing the crocodile, and come out the other side unscathed!
2. One example of this devotion involved the towns of Oxyrhynchus and Cynopolis. In Oxyrhynchus the people revered the oxyrhynchus fish. In Cynopolis the people revered dogs, and they ate these fish. The people of Oxyrhynchus asked the people of Cynopolis to stop eating their sacred fish, but they refused. In retaliation the people of Oxyrhynchus killed, roasted, and ate the sacred dogs of Cynopolis. This insult started a civil war between the towns.

## 2. Cat Worship

1. Some characters in Egyptian mythology are known by more than one name. For example, Bastet is sometimes called Bast, Ra is sometimes called Re, and Apep is sometimes called Apophis.
2. This is from Herodotus's *Histories*. The second of the nine volumes is about the customs of Egypt.

## 3. A Second Chance at Life

1. Depictions of gods and goddesses varied. Sometimes Isis was shown with wings, but sometimes she wasn't. The god Thoth was sometimes depicted as a baboon, sometimes as an ibis.
2. X rays of some cat and kitten mummies have shown that their neck bones were separated. This means that they were strangled. Apparently some cats were sacrificed and then mummified. But that contradicts the reverence the average Egyptian felt for cats. Perhaps these sacrifices were performed by priests as part of a temple ritual.

## 4. Bubastis

1. Because much of what we know about ancient Egypt comes from literature originally written in Greek, many pharaohs are better known by their Greek names. For example, Cheops is the Greek name of the pharaoh Khufu, and Chephren is the Greek name of the pharaoh Khafre.

## 6. Death of a Religion

1. William Martin Conway, in his book *Dawn of Art in the Ancient World,* said of the cat cemetery, "The discovery meant wealth for somebody, probably not the finder, but the head-man of the village." In 1888 exporting Egyptian antiquities was illegal. But that rarely stopped anyone from doing it. Every antiquity had its price, and the local people knew it. Those involved in selling these cat mummies apparently thought that the mummies' monetary value was more important than their historical value.

# Names and Terms

*Alexander* (al-ig-ZAN-der) *the Great*: Lived 356–323 B.C. As leader of Macedonia he conquered Greece, Egypt, and the Persian Empire, and founded the city of Alexandria.

*amulet* (AM-you-let): In ancient Egypt, a carved or molded object usually worn as a pendant or placed on a dead body; believed to have magical powers that protected the wearer from evil.

*Anubis* (uh-NOO-bis): The god of funerals and embalming; portrayed as a black jackal or a man with a jackal's head.

*Apep* (uh-PEP): A giant serpent who fought Ra each night; a symbol of evil and darkness.

*Bastet* (bast-ET): The goddess who personified the beneficial power of the sun, protector of pregnant women, protector of people from disease and evil; portrayed as a woman with a cat's head.

*Bubastis* (boo-BAS-tis): Ancient city in the eastern Nile Delta; center of the cult of Bastet and home of the pharaohs of the Twenty-second Dynasty.

*Cambyses* (kam-BYE-seez): King of Persia 529–521 B.C., son of Cyrus the Great; conquered Egypt in 525 B.C.

*Cheops* (KEE-ops): Greek name of Khufu (KOO-foo), second pharaoh of the Fourth Dynasty, for whom the Great Pyramid at Giza was built.

*Chephren* (KEF-run): Greek name of Khafre (KAHF-ray), fourth pharaoh of the Fourth Dynasty, for whom the second-largest pyramid at Giza was built.

*Cyrus* (SYE-rus) *the Great*: King of Persia around 558–529 B.C., founder of the Persian Empire.

*dynasty* (DYE-nuh-stee): A family of rulers that maintains power for several generations.

*Herodotus* (huh-ROD-uh-tus): Greek historian of the fifth century B.C.; called "the father of history."

*ibis* (EYE-bis): A long-billed wading bird associated with the god Thoth and revered by the Egyptians as an enemy of poisonous snakes.

*ichneumon* (ick-NOO-mun): A mongoose that the Egyptians revered for destroying crocodile eggs and snakes.

*Isis* (EYE-sis): Wife of Osiris; helped him civilize Egypt.

*Juvenal* (JOO-vuh-nul): Lived A.D. 60?–?140, full name Decimus Junius Juvenalis; Roman satirical poet who attacked the politics and society of the Roman Empire, including Egypt.

*mummification* (mum-i-fi-KAY-shun): The process of embalming and drying a body to preserve it.

*Nile*: The world's longest river; the center of the world and the source of all life for the ancient Egyptians.

*Osiris* (oh-SYE-ris): The god whose death and resurrection symbolized the fertility of nature; usually portrayed as a mummy.

*pharaoh* (FAIR-oh): Literal meaning "great house," referring to the Egyptian royal palace and eventually to the palace and the king.

*Ptolemy* (TAHL-uh-mee): The name of fifteen Greek rulers of Egypt from 304–30 B.C.

*Ra* (RAH): The sun god, who sailed across the sky each day.

*Sekhmet* (SEK-met): The lion-headed goddess of the destructive heat of the sun.

*Sheshonk* (SHE-shongk): Libyan pharaoh and founder of the Twenty-second Dynasty; made Bubastis a major city.

*totem* (TOE-tum): An animal or object serving as the emblem of a clan.

*Tutankhamen* (toot-ahngk-AH-mun): A pharaoh of the Eighteenth Dynasty who ruled in the fourteenth century B.C. and whose tomb was discovered in 1922, the only ancient Egyptian royal tomb discovered intact.

# Selected Bibliography

Asterisks (*) indicate books of special interest to young readers

* Baines, John, and Jaromír Málek. *Atlas of Ancient Egypt.* New York: Facts on File, 1988.

Beadle, Muriel. *The Cat.* New York: Simon & Schuster, 1979.

Bratton, F. Gladstone. *A History of Egyptian Archaeology.* London: Robert Hale, 1967.

Budge, E. A. Wallis. *The Book of the Dead.* London: Arkana, 1985.

————. *Egyptian Magic.* New York: Benjamin Blom, 1971.

Clement of Alexandria. *The Writings of Clement of Alexandria.* Rev. William Wilson, trans. Edinburgh: T. & T. Clark, 1869.

Conway, William Martin. *Dawn of Art in the Ancient World.* New York: Macmillan & Co., 1891.

Cotterell, Arthur, ed. *The Encyclopedia of Ancient Civilizations.* London: The Rainbird Publishing Group, 1980.

* Dale-Green, Patricia. *Cult of the Cat.* Boston: Houghton Mifflin Company, 1963.

D'Auria, Sue, *et al. Mummies & Magic.* Boston: Museum of Fine Art, Boston, 1988.

David, Rosalie. *Cult of the Sun.* London: J. M. Dent & Sons, 1980.

Diodorus Siculus. *The Antiquities of Egypt: A Translation with Notes of Book I of the "Library of History" of Diodorus Siculus.* Edwin Murphy, trans. New Brunswick, NJ: Transaction Publishers, 1990.

* El Mahdy, Christine. *Mummies, Myth and Magic in Ancient Egypt.* New York: Thames & Hudson, 1989.

Erman, Adolf. *A Handbook of Egyptian Religion.* New York: E. P. Dutton & Co., 1907.

Fagan, Brian M. *The Rape of the Nile.* New York: Charles Scribner's Sons, 1975.

Gershevitch, Ilya, ed. *The Cambridge History of Iran.* London: Cambridge University Press, 1985.

Herodotus. *The History of Herodotus.* George Rawlinson, trans. New York: Tudor Publishing Company, 1939.

Howey, M. Oldfield. *The Cat in the Mysteries of Religion and Magic.* New York: Arthur Richmond Company, 1955.

James, T. G. H., ed. *Excavating in Egypt: The Egyptian Exploration Society 1882–1982.* Chicago: University of Chicago Press, 1982.

Juvenal. *Satires.* Jerome Mazzaro, trans. Ann Arbor, MI: University of Michigan Press, 1965.

Leca, Ange-Pierre. *The Egyptian Way of Death: Mummies and the Cult of the Immortal.* Garden City, NY: Doubleday & Company, 1981.

Maspero, G. *History of Egypt, Chaldea, Syria, Babylon, and Assyria.* London: The Grolier Society, 1903.

Mercatante, Anthony S. *Who's Who in Egyptian Mythology.* New York: Clarkson N. Potter, 1978.

Naville, Edouard. *Eighth Memoir of the Egypt Exploration Fund: Bubastis.* London: Messrs. Kegan Paul, Trench, Trübner & Co., 1891.

Polyaenus. *Polyaenus's Stratagems of War.* R. Shepherd, trans. Chicago: Ares Publishers, 1974.

Rappoport, S. *History of Egypt from 330 BC to the Present.* London: The Grolier Society, 1904.

Sayer, Angela. *The Encyclopedia of the Cat.* New York: Crescent Books, 1979.

Sharpe, Samuel. *The History of Egypt.* London: George Bell & Sons, 1885.

Spencer, A. J. *Death in Ancient Egypt.* Harmondsworth, England: Penguin Books, 1986.

*The Times* of London. "Nineteen Tons of Cats," February 4, 1890.

———. "Mummy Cats," February 11, 1890.

Wilkinson, Sir J. Gardner. *The Manners and Customs of the Ancient Egyptians.* London: John Murray, 1878.

# Index

Afterlife, 18–20, 45–46
Alexander the Great, 37, 48, 52
Alexandria, 48, 52
Amasis, 33–34
Amenemhet I, 26
Amulets, 13, 46, 52
Animals and religion, 1–6, 12, 25, 29, 37–40, 50. *See also* Cats; Gods and goddesses
Antiquities, 40–44, 51
Archaeology, 26, 40, 43–44

Baboons, 47, 50
Beetles, 3, 47
Beni Hasan, 1, 23, 28, 40
Bubastis, 12, 23–29, 48, 52, 53

Cambyses, 32–34, 37–38, 48, 52
Canopic jars, 45
Cats
    Bastet and, 10–13, 23–29, 47, 50, 52
    cemeteries for, 23, 27–29, 40–42, 51
    death of, 6, 14, 28, 37
    ka of, 20, 23
    mummies of, 1, 14, 20, 23, 28, 49, 50; as antiquities, 40–44, 51
    sacred, 3–14, 25, 37–40, 43, 50
    sculptures and statues of, 13, 23
    usefulness of, 7
    as "weapons," 37, 41
Cheops, 26, 48, 51, 52
Chephren, 26, 48, 51, 52
Christianity, 39–40
Clans, 1–2, 25, 53
Clement of Alexandria, 39
Coffins, 23, 45–46
Cremation, 28
Crocodiles, 4, 39, 50, 53
Cynopolis, 50
Cyrus the Great, 32, 48, 52

Desiccation, 45–46
Diodorus Siculus, 4, 6, 50
Dogs, 37, 50

Egypt
    Alexander's conquest of, 37, 48, 52
    Arab conquest of, 40, 48
    Persian conquest of, 29, 32–37, 48, 52
    and Romans, 6, 38, 48, 53
Embalming, 18–19, 45–46, 47, 52

Giza, 26, 48, 52
Gods and goddesses
    animals associated with, 3–6, 47. *See also* Animals and religion; Cats, Bastet and
    Anubis, 3, 47, 52
    Apep, 7, 50, 52
    Bastet, 10–13, 23–29, 47, 50, 52
    Buto, 47
    Geb, 47
    Horus, 47
    Isis, 16–18, 47, 50, 53
    Khepera, 47
    Nekhebet, 47
    offerings and vows to, 4, 13, 29, 50
    Osiris, 16–18, 47, 53
    Ra, 7, 12, 47, 50, 52, 53
    Sekhmet, 10, 53
    Set, 16–18
    Taweret, 47
    Thoth, 47, 50, 53

Herodotus, 14, 25, 27–29, 50, 52
Hieroglyphics, 44

Ibises, 2, 3, 37, 47, 50, 53
Ichneumons, 4, 50, 53
Islam, 40, 48

Jackals, 3, 47, 52
Juvenal, 38, 53

Ka, 18–19, 23

Lions, 10–11

Masks, 20, 46
Mummification
    of cats, 14, 20
    of humans, 19, 45–46
Myths and legends, 7, 12, 16–18, 50

Napoleon Bonaparte, 43–44
Naville, Edouard, 26, 28
Nile River, 3, 4, 16, 25, 29, 50, 53

Osorkon II and III, 27

Persian Empire, 32–37, 52
Pelusium, 33–37
Phanes, 33–34
Priests, 4, 39, 50
Psammetichus III, 34
Ptolemies, 6, 37, 48, 53
Pyramids, 1, 26, 45, 48, 52

Roman Empire, 4, 68; 53
Rosetta Stone, 44

Sheshonk I, 12, 27, 48, 53
Snakes and serpents, 2, 7, 39, 47, 52, 53

Tel Basta, 25
Temples and shrines, 4, 13, 39–40, 50
    Bastet's, 12–13, 25–27
Thebes, 23
Totems, 1–3, 25, 53
Tutankhamen, 44, 46, 48, 53

Zagazig, 25